DANCES *for* CHRISTMAS

BOOK 2

6 Intermediate Christmas Favorites Arranged in Dance Styles

CATHERINE ROLLIN

One of the rewards of composing music is knowing that my message is universal. People of all nations and backgrounds enjoy music, and no translation is needed to understand the emotions communicated through the language of music. I witnessed this in Japan when I presented my duet books, *Dances for Two, Books 1* and *2*. I saw students and teachers not only enjoying my music, but also getting up and dancing! It occurred to me that dance, like music, is also an international language. This experience led me to write two solo collections in dance styles, *Dancing on the Keys, Books 1* and *2*.

When the editors at Alfred Publishing suggested that I add Christmas pieces arranged in dance styles to my growing body of work with a dance theme, I thought this was a wonderful idea. What could be more perfect than combining these two international languages—music and dance—to celebrate this most joyous time of the year? In addition, several of the pieces have optional percussion parts for more rhythmic fun!

I wish all teachers, students and their families a beautiful holiday season, filled with joy, music and dance.

Merry Christmas!

Contents

D1275295

JOLLY OLD SAINT NICHOLAS
(Gigue)

Traditional
Arr. Catherine Rollin

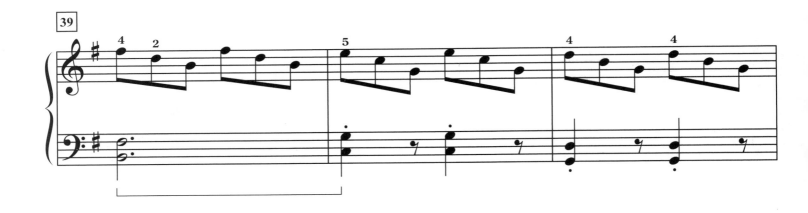

WHAT CHILD IS THIS?
(Paso Doble)

Optional Percussion:

Measures 1–15 and 63–67

Traditional English Melody
Arr. Catherine Rollin

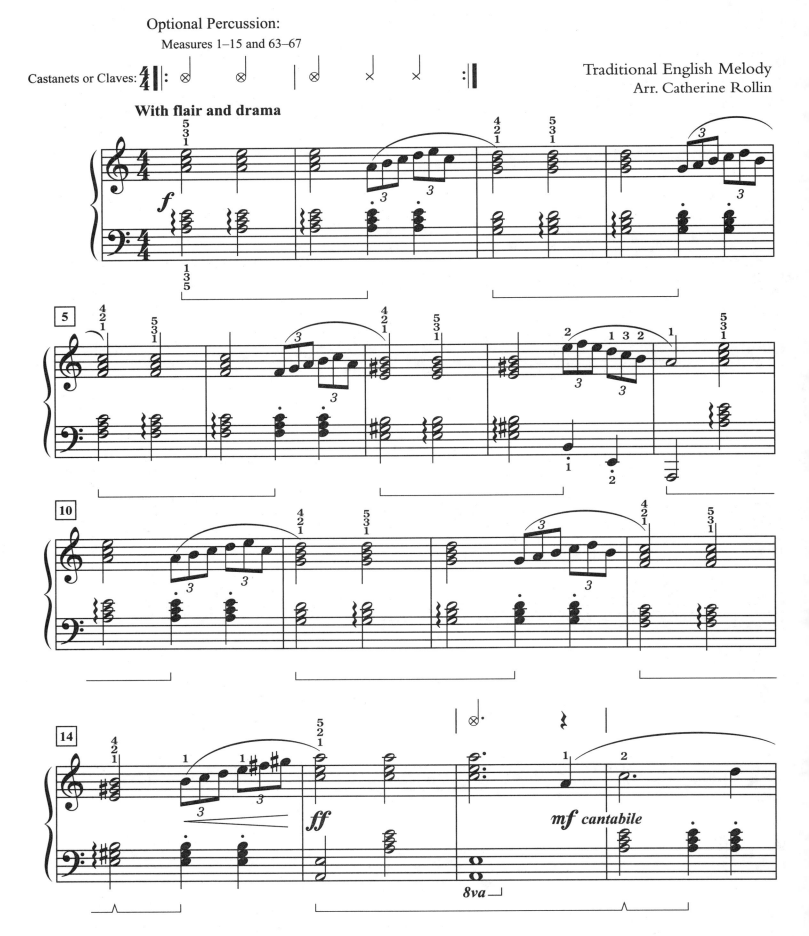

7

Measures 68–70

* Play beat 1 staccato, but hold the pedal down until beat 3.

THE TWELVE DAYS OF CHRISTMAS
(Gavotte)

Traditional
Arr. Catherine Rollin

12

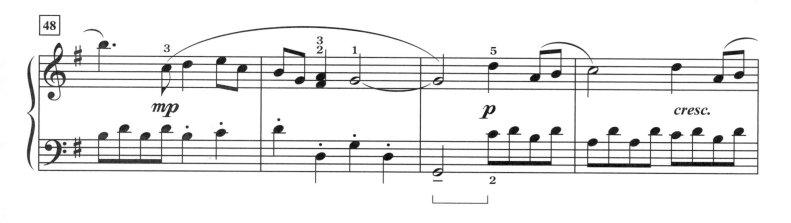

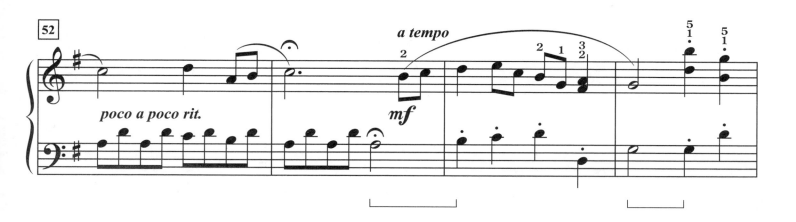

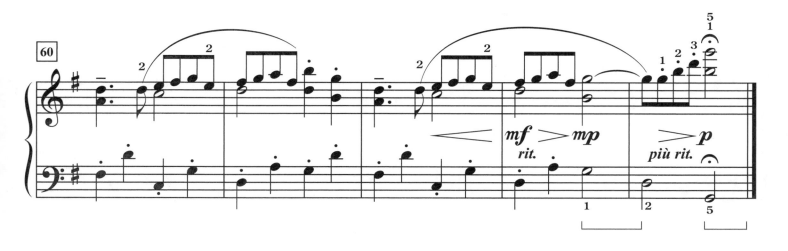

THE LITTLE DRUMMER BOY
(Bolero)

Optional Percussion:

Words and Music by Harry Simeone,
Henry Onorati and Katherine Davis
Arr. Catherine Rollin

SILENT NIGHT
(Waltz)

Franz Grüber
Catherine Rollin

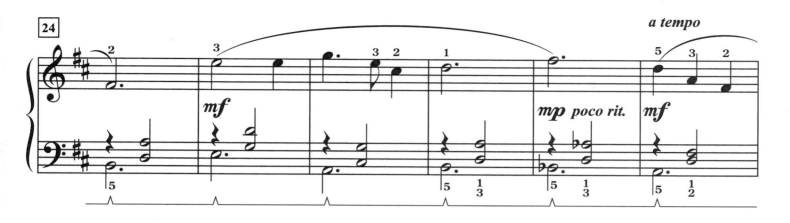

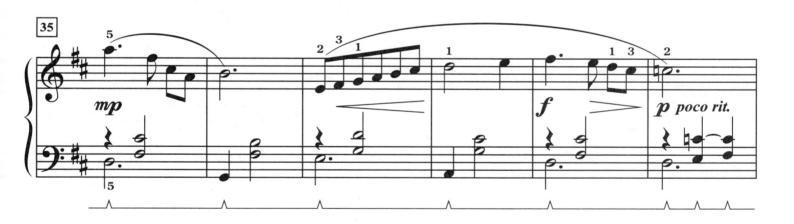

Winter Wonderlands
(Salsa)

Words by Dick Smith
Music by Felix Bernard
Arr. Catherine Rollin

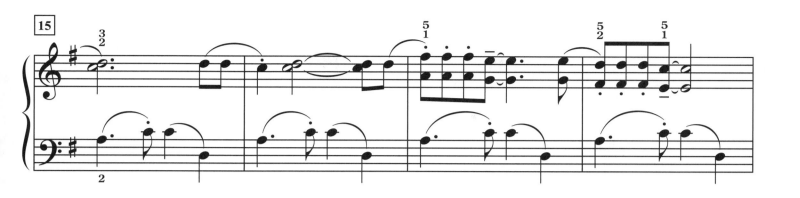

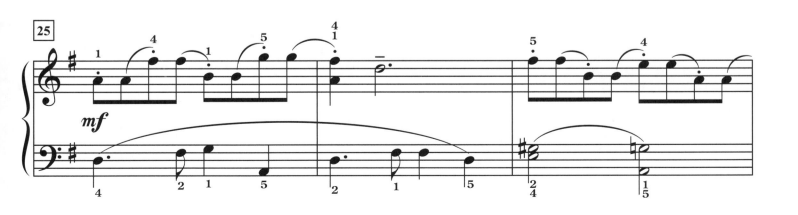

Measure 40